MW01242281

Made in the USA
Middletown, DE
09 August 2022

70892753R00068